I AND My Seed Will Thrive
By Racheal Odoy

Giant Publishing Company
Lincoln, Nebraska USA

2019 by Racheal Odoy

Published by Giant Publishing Company
Post Office Box 6455
Lincoln, NE 68506
www.giantpublishingcompany.com

Printed in the United States of America

All rights reserved. No part of this publication may be used or reproduced in any form or by any electronic or mechanical means, including information storage and retrieval systems, without permission in writing from the publisher.

All scriptures are from the King James Version of the Bible, unless otherwise noted.

ISBN: 978-0-9995873-5-5

Odoy, Racheal
I AND My Seed Will Thrive
Non-fiction/Racheal Odoy
    1. Non-fiction-Christianity
    2. Bible commentary
    3. Self-help

Also by Racheal Odoy:

You Need a Jonathan - Copyright 2018, Giant Publishing Company

I dedicate this book to my husband, Larry Odoy, and to my two boys, who have supported me all through the process as I was writing it. And also, to the church family of No-Limits International Christian Center.

Table of Contents

Introduction

Poem

Prayer

Chapter 1: The seed ……………..................…..Page 13
(a) The potential of a seed

Chapter 2: Disconnect and denounce covenants……...
…………………………………………………..Page 19
(a) Family covenants
(b) Relationship covenants
(c) Soul tie
(d) Transfer of spirits
Prayer

Chapter 3: Words have power……...…………..Page 31
(a) Avoid negative statements
Prayer
(b) Speak positively
Prayer
(c) Never give up
(d) Gain trust from your child
Prayer

Chapter 4: Be grateful ………………....……...Page 54
(a) Enough is never enough
(b) Do not compare children

Prayer

Chapter 5: Prayer direction........................ ...Page 66
(a) Family prayer altar
Prayer
(b) Get a prayer partner
(c) Steps of selecting a prayer partner
 Prayer
(d) Write a list of expectations
(e) Pray for other families
(f) Pray for your pastor
(g) Honor the church leadership
(h) God's word is true

Chapter 6: Prayer groups ....Page 99
(a) Mothers prayer group
(b) Marrieds prayer group
(c) Youth prayer group
(d) Singles prayer group
(e) The power of your seed
(f) How to speak over your seed

Introduction

Who wakes up and says, "I have never been a child?" It all begins from the day you were conceived in your mother's womb. She may have known the day she conceived you or not, but the fact remains that she carried you in her womb for nine months. I believe that no man or woman was conceived by mistake, as some people may say. Every person is born for a purpose, and that is according to God.

Jeremiah 1:5: Before I formed thee in the belly I knew thee; and before thou camest forth out of the womb I sanctified thee, and I ordained thee a prophet unto the nations.

My inspiration for writing this book is based on a true story of a girl child who constantly cried. She sought for help while asking herself so many questions, and the main one was, "WHY ME?" I realized that this girl had done no crime, but was a victim of circumstances which she had no control over. And as she grew up, she started realizing her purpose for living and pursuing it on her own. Instead of focusing on her sorrow and pain she decided to focus on how she could overcome it, and how to get to that place she always dreamed of.

With patience, persistence and diligence she made it, and even got married and had children. One thing she purposed to do in her children's lives was to see them grow up and become responsible in society. And in so doing, she taught her children to always put God first in everything. For she was looking ahead to a generation which will make a difference.

Proverbs 22:6: Train up a child in the way he should go: and when he is old, he will not depart from it.

In this book you are going to be guided as well as be encouraged on how to constantly pray for yourself and your children, and to never focus on your children's mistakes or give up on them. You are going to learn how to work with them to create a great difference in their lives, no matter their ages. As a parent, God trusted you with his gift of that child. Children are your biggest responsibility on earth.

As you read, you will get healing in your inner man who has been hurting for a while, and also get answers to some of those questions you have been asking yourself.

Remember, you were once a child, and it's time to create a difference in you and around you. I want to tell you that in every man there's a boy, and in every woman there's a girl. You are a child of God. Be ready to receive healing, transformation and freedom of the unseen inner man as you read this book.

Psalm 127:3-5: Lo, children are an heritage of the Lord: and the fruit of the womb is his reward. As arrows are in the hand of a mighty man; so are children of the youth. Happy is the man that hath his quiver full of them: they shall not be ashamed, but they shall speak with the enemies in the gate.

Why Me (Tears of a Child)

Every single day she looked outside the window
Wishing the clouds would speak to her
Wondering the reason as to why she was born
Her inside cried louder than her outside
Those around her called her strong and brave
Nobody cared to know exactly what was happening inside of her
She would smile constantly and work hard each day
Praying to see herself one day smiling inside
Just like the outside seemed to everyone.

Not a single day would she allow those around her to see her tears
But deep in the night she would face the wall and cry
Asking God one question: 'Why me? Why me?'
She prayed constantly telling God of how she felt
Promising him to make a difference in the lives of others if he helped her
Those around her would say to her one thing:
'You are really blessed to know how to pray.'
Little did they know that she was seeking for something bigger than what they could see.

The tides began to change in her life as she pursued hard for her dreams

Finished her school, graduated and thinking it was now better, but it became bitter. She never lost hope but continued to pray. Finally-
God answered her prayer, she got married, had children and decided to make her struggling history into a life-changing story. Teaching the word of God and helping those who seem hopeless and helpless by encouraging them.

Prayer (read it loudly)

Father, I come to you in the name of your son Jesus Christ. So much has been going on, but I do not know even where to begin from, because my life has been full of many questions that have never been answered.

The burden in my heart is way too much for me to carry, and I know not of a man who can carry this off my heart. That is why I choose to come in your presence and seek for help, my God.

I am tired of feeling heavy and going through pain that has no cure by medication. That's why I call unto you as it is written in:

Jeremiah 33:3: Call unto me, and I will answer thee, and show thee great and mighty things, which thou knowest not.

My Lord, I commit my whole family into your hands and cover them in the blood of Jesus Christ, for no weapon formed against them shall prosper, in Jesus' mighty name.

God, you are the giver of life, and nothing will ever take away the gift of life you have given to me. I surrender all to you Lord; be my guide and my friend.

Father, I shall fear no evil nor allow the enemy to destroy me and all that is connected to me in Jesus' mighty name. I put all my trust in you.

As it is written in Deuteronomy 31:6: Be strong and of a good courage, fear not, nor be afraid of them: for the Lord thy God, he it is that doth go with thee; he will not fail thee, nor forsake thee.

I know, Lord, you will never leave me nor forsake me because your word says I Kings 8:57: The LORD our God be with us, as he was with our fathers: let him not leave us, nor forsake us.

Chapter 1: The seed

The principle of the seed is seen right from the beginning of God's creation. For a continuation of anything, there must be a seed that produces a fruit which produces a seed, and the line continues.

Every seed carries the DNA of the original fruit, because it's a continuation. God gave a command to every living creature that moves and all the birds of the air to be fruitful, produce after their kind and multiply, which makes it possible for a lion to give birth to a lion, while a dog gives birth to a dog.

Genesis 1:20-31: And God said, Let the waters bring forth abundantly the moving creature that hath life, and fowl that may fly above the earth in the open firmament of heaven. And God created great whales, and every living creature that moveth, which the waters brought forth abundantly, after their kind, and every winged fowl after his kind: and God saw that it was good. And God blessed them, saying, Be fruitful, and multiply, and fill the waters in the seas, and let fowl multiply in the earth. And the evening and the morning were the fifth day. And God said, Let the earth bring forth the living creature after his kind, cattle, and creeping thing, and beast of the earth after his kind: and it was so. And God made the beast of the earth after his kind, and cattle after their kind, and every thing that creepeth upon the earth after his kind: and God saw that it was good. And God said, Let us make man in our image, after our likeness: and let them have dominion over the fish of the sea, and over the fowl of the air, and over the cattle, and over all the earth, and over every creeping thing that creepeth upon the earth. So God created man in his own image, in the image of God created he him; male and female created he them. And God blessed them, and God said unto them, Be fruitful, and multiply, and replenish the earth, and subdue it: and have dominion over the fish of the sea, and over the fowl of the air, and over every living thing that moveth upon the earth. And God said, Behold, I have given you every herb bearing seed, which is upon the face of all the earth, and every tree, in the which is the fruit of a tree yielding seed; to you it shall be for meat. And to every beast of the earth, and to every fowl of the air, and to everything that creepeth upon the earth, wherein there is life, I have given every green herb for meat: and it was so. And God saw everything that he had made, and, behold, it was very good. And the evening and the morning were the sixth day.

The potential of a seed

Every seed has a potential to grow into a fruit, and every fruit has the potential to produce a seed or seeds. If a tree that carries fruits is cut down, yet the roots are still firm in the ground, the chances of this tree to grow again are 99%. And why? Simply because there are roots that are holding it firm. And as time goes on, especially if there is the right atmosphere, that specific tree will start to grow again.

Therefore, it is very important to always create the right atmosphere for any tree that carries branches, whose branches carry fruits, and the fruits carry inside of them seeds.

Jesus said in John 15:5: I am the vine, ye are the branches: He that abideth in me, and I in him, the same bringeth forth much fruit: for without me ye can do nothing.

What Jesus meant was, as individuals we must be in position to accept him as our Lord and savior by confessing our sins, asking for forgiveness, and inviting him in our hearts. And by so doing (he abiding in us), we will be in position to produce fruits.

Colossians 1:10: That ye might walk worthy of the Lord unto all pleasing, being fruitful in every good work, and increasing in the knowledge of God.

Galatians 5:22-23: But the fruit of the Spirit is love, joy, peace, longsuffering, gentleness, goodness, faith, Meekness, temperance: against such there is no law.

Every believer's fruitfulness must be in position to produce fruits. This is so that the way you carry yourself should attract so many people in the kingdom of God.

And, I believe this should start with your household. As a family it is very important to always live and stand steadily on the word of God, making the word into a daily bread by having family devotions. Whenever a family walks by the word it is very rare to find them divided, because the word of God keeps them together. And the seeds/children of that family will grow up in the fear of God, becoming potential fruits, which in the long run as they grow and also get families, they will be able to produce very good seeds, and the lineage continues.

Proverbs 22:6: Train up a child in the way he should go: and when he is old, he will not depart from it.

We can see this in the book of Exodus when God called Moses while he kept the flock of Jethro his father-in-law, the priest of Midian. God told Moses: *I am the God of thy father, the God of Abraham, the God of Isaac, and the God of Jacob.*

God himself referred to a lineage of descendants that walked with him. And since the people in bondage were descendants of these people, God remembered them at such a time when he identified a man called Moses who also was brought up in the palace of the Egyptian Pharaoh by a woman (his mother) who told him of his true identity. And by God referring to Moses' descendants, he was truly identifying himself as none other than he who was with Moses' forefathers, as the same one who is talking to him now. So, God called Moses to rescue the seed of Abraham, Isaac and Jacob, for it was time for them to get their freedom from slavery in Egypt.

Exodus 3:1-8: Now Moses kept the flock of Jethro his father in law, the priest of Midian: and he led the flock to the backside of the desert, and came to the mountain of God, even to Horeb. And the angel of the Lord appeared unto him in a flame of fire out of the midst of a bush: and he looked, and, behold, the bush burned with fire, and the bush was not consumed. And Moses said, I will now turn aside, and see this great sight, why the bush is not burnt. And when the Lord saw that he turned aside to see, God called unto him out of the midst of the bush, and said, Moses, Moses. And he said, Here am I. And he said, Draw not nigh hither: put off thy shoes from off thy feet, for the place whereon thou standest is holy ground. Moreover he said, I am the God of thy father, the God of Abraham, the God of Isaac, and the God of Jacob. And Moses hid his face; for he was afraid to look upon God. And the Lord said, I have surely seen the affliction of my people which are in Egypt, and have heard their cry by reason of their taskmasters; for I know their sorrows; And I am come down to deliver them out of the hand of the Egyptians, and to bring them up out of that land unto a good land and a large, unto a land flowing with milk and honey; unto the place of the Canaanites, and the Hittites, and the Amorites, and the Perizzites, and the Hivites, and the Jebusites.

God will never give up on his true seed, and you are a seed of Abraham, our father of faith, who walked with God in obedience and patience. It therefore calls for you never to give up on yourself or your children, because inside of you and your seed, there is a potential of multiplication.

Chapter 2: Disconnect and denounce covenants

The term "covenant" is of Latin origin (con venire), meaning a coming together. It presupposes two or more parties who come together to agree on promises, stipulations, privileges, and responsibilities.

It can be written or verbal. Marriage is a good illustration of a covenant, for a man and woman choose to enter into a relationship with one another and make promises to one another. They agree verbally, then they are given a written paper, a marriage certificate, which affirms the words they have spoken. In one way or another there is always a point of contact that keeps the parties involved together. Things like names, rings, bangles, clothes, badges, tattoos, a common word spoken for identity, or specific sign language for identity.

A covenant binds you together with the party that you made it with. Some can be easy to break off from, but some can be almost next to impossible, depending on the terms and conditions involved in the covenant. But one thing I know, it is written:

Mathew 19:26: But Jesus beheld them, and said unto them, With men this is impossible; but with God all things are possible.

The covenants that am going to open your eyes to here as you read are either known or unknown to you. That is why am going to describe them in a simpler manner to help you identify for yourself whether you are involved or not. I am going to be referring to your everyday living, which you probably least expected had any impact on you or your children.

I am going to concentrate more on family covenants and relationship covenants that always impact our lives when we are not even aware that they do. To your eyes they may not mean so much, but yet in reality, it is affecting you or your children and probably is the reason why you have been having so many questions, like, "Why me?"

And remember (unless you realize the problem), you cannot get a solution to what you do not know. (You cannot get treatment for cancer unless you know you have cancer.)

I assure you, you are going to realize the root problem of your struggle as you read, and even deal with it once and for all. It's your time of freedom.

Family covenants

Most families have covenants that were made decades back, and yet the current generation knows nothing about them. Family covenants are not easy to break off from, because people usually get so attached to their families that they never realize the reason as to why there is a commonality of a certain thing among all family members.

It's going to take you as a person to look beyond the physical and pay deep attention to the unseen root behavior, yet recognized by so many. The problem comes when you see the problem surfacing, yet you fail to identify the root cause.

Most of these family covenants are usually verbal when parents make statements which are careless. For instance, a father can make a statement like: "All my children will be like me," not putting into consideration the weaknesses he is struggling with, like alcohol, or simply being a vagabond.

This is where you as a child of such a father find yourself still struggling to stop craving for alcohol, and it's so hard for you, and the same thing is happening to your child.

When you recognize that it's not just you failing to stop being an alcoholic, but there is a force behind you that pushes you to continually drink alcohol, then know that you are close to being free. You have looked beyond the problem and know the root cause.

Now it is going to be easy for you to disconnect yourself and your children from that covenant that was made by your father and has been having control over you.

In some families there are tangible things that are usually passed on from generation to generation and by the time you have it, you do not even know the words that were spoken over that particular thing, neither do you know the reason as to why it is being passed on from generation to generation. And here you are finding yourself in a situation that you have no explanation of how it came about.

In 2017 I met with a family that needed prayer, and all of them were complaining of one common thing, which was headaches. They informed me that their grandfather died in his sleep, but the previous night he was complaining of a severe headache. Immediately I had to connect with the Holy Spirit to find out the reason why they were all complaining of the same thing. And by that time the oldest girl in this family was very sick.

God, being so loving and faithful, caused me to notice that the baby was wearing a necklace. And so, I asked that they should remove it. All of them said they cannot, because in their family every child is given that special necklace, and they can only remove it when they are six years old. I insisted, and then told them that there is a curse that is being passed on from generation to generation, and that has been for a long time the cause of their problem. It was the reason as to why the family was going through so many problems.

After I revealed to them the root problem, a few family members decided to denounce and disconnect themselves from all the family covenants. And I witnessed their lives changing - glory be to God.

You may be reading this testimony and all you are saying is, "How do I even know the root cause of all my problems?" Do not be discouraged; I am going to help you here as you read, and you are going to be free.

Relationship covenants

Here I am going to focus more on the relationships you may have probably had in the past with that specific woman or man. And note, I am talking about the relationships between a man and woman, girlfriend and boyfriend. It is very sad that so many people do not know the impact past relationships may have had on them, that even their current relationship is being affected. A good number of people will say it is in the past, but one thing I know: the past has such a great impact on the present. That is why we ought to rectify some of our past. That can only be done through accepting Jesus Christ as your Lord and savior and dying to self each and every day, while walking in God's ways and bearing fruits that will produce seeds, as we expand on the kingdom of God.

Allow me to first of all ask you a question. Did you and your ex agree on certain things (promises) as to what will keep you together forever, and you are no longer together? Secondly, did you have any sexual intimacy? What was your answer? Okay! Then continue reading and learn how things we usually take for granted have such a great impact on us unknowingly.

A case in scenario is this lady I met (name withheld). She was married for nine years and had no child. She and her husband had tried everything to have children, but no success. They prayed and fasted and waited for the next month to see if she was pregnant, but nothing. So, they decided to go to a gynecologist to do some procedures, and none of them were successful. And by the time she met me, she said she had given up and would wait until God answered her. When, she had no idea.

So, I sat with her and listened more as she was narrating the frustration she was going through because her husband had had a child with another woman before he met her and married her.

I prayed for her and as I was praying, I was led by the Holy Spirit to ask her about her past relationships - if she had a child and was keeping it as a secret. The answer will shock you. She said, "Not really." Seriously; 'not really' meant she had, and something had happened. So, she went ahead and told me. When she was sixteen years old, she had a boyfriend, and they were together for three years, and within that time she happened to get pregnant. I was like, "Uhhhh..." So, I asked her to go ahead and tell me. She said she agreed with the boyfriend to terminate the pregnancy, and by then she was three months' pregnant. So, they did, and afterwards, they agreed that they will never have children until they both agreed on it. Immediately I knew that was the root problem, because they didn't stay together for long after that. And here she was, wanting to get pregnant, and she couldn't. And she did not know that the covenant she made with her ex-boyfriend was stopping her from conceiving.

I laid hands on her stomach and prayed and cancelled the covenant she made years back, and I also asked her to ask God for forgiveness for the abortion she had, killing an innocent child. And with God being good and loving, it took her only one month, and she conceived and had a baby boy. Glory be to God.

The power of a covenant/agreement! It is very easy for someone to get in a covenant when all they see is the convenience of the current situation, yet the impact will always be there, no matter how long. It only takes the grace of God to break strongholds in a covenant, especially ungodly covenants.

There are also cases when lovers (man and woman) agree on loving each other forever and promise to never let anyone get in between them. But as time goes on, they disagree and break up, and each moves on and finds another person and falls in love. These are the cases you always come across, and people are fighting because of their ex who keeps coming back.

I have witnessed marriages breaking up because of the ex-boyfriend who shows up, and the woman starts cheating on her husband. And in this day and age with the technology of phones having passwords and different apps, so much happens that marriages become bitter instead of better. And if such a couple had children, they become the victims of circumstances because separation and sometimes divorce comes in, which causes the children to grow up with divided attention in such a way that they are struggling to identify who of the two parents loves them more. And it doesn't end there; you will find the same thing repeating itself among the children and the children's children, now becoming generational. And look where it started from - one of the parents having a covenant/strong tie with a lover, whom they did not end up getting married to.

And sometimes it does not stop at making promises. Some people, if not 85% of the people, who get in relationships (man and woman) usually get intimate and have sex. Sex itself is a covenant which binds two souls together.

Soul tie

This is a spiritual connection between two people who have been intimate with each other physically and emotionally. Sex is good, but only with the right partner, in marriage (man and woman).

When we have sex, our brains get this chemical known as dopamine. It's like an addiction. It memorizes the feeling which was good, and you always want to get that feeling of that particular thing. It's exciting. Like people who get addicted to gambling, alcohol or drugs, their satisfaction is when they get these things, and it gets difficult for them to break free from such addictions, because it's within.

Soul tie is more serious than you think. You will find that if you had sex with someone, that feeling of how it was remains in someone's head. It is so addictive that there are some people who can enjoy sex with their spouses only when they have an imagination of the past sex experience they had in the past relationship.

Amazingly it doesn't matter what kind of experience a person had when they got intimate with another person - those feelings are so strong. Even when someone was raped, that ugly feeling sticks in the mind, so that when it comes to sex, all they have is dislike for it.

I know of a lady who was raped by her closest uncle from the age of ten to sixteen. She suffered emotionally so much that even counselling did not help. The effect it had on her was terrible; she had so much hatred for men that even talking to them was difficult.

I was ministering in a conference, and she came to me and fell on her face crying. That was after I gave her a prophetic word that she needed to forgive her uncle and allow God to bring healing in her soul so that she could move on. You could see the pain she was carrying inside of her, and it tore her apart for years, to the point that she never considered getting married or having children. She feared that if she gave birth to a girl, someone might defile her daughter in the same way. It was so hard for her.

I give God all the glory and honor, and surely God reveals to redeem. By the touch of the Holy Spirit, she fell under the power and received healing. At the end of the conference she came to me and said, "Thank you; I feel very light."

Intimacy (sexual) carries so much impact on your life, either positively or negatively, so you ought to be very careful who you get intimate with, because it goes with you everywhere you go.

When two people (man and woman) get intimate sexually, there is something that takes place which is called transfer of spirits. Have you heard of people looking at a married couple (man and woman) together and they say that they look alike? It's because these two people constantly agree on things, both physically and emotionally. They literally start having the same preferences for things. When you ask one a question, the way he/she answers will not be different from the other one's answer.

Transfer of spirits

This is when an evil spirit which is in one person moves and enters another person, and it happens in different ways. One of them is through sexual intimacy. Other ways are clothes, jewelry and initiations in cults or tribes.

Remember, covenants can be made verbally or physically, depending on what kind of covenant you are getting yourself involved in. But there is hope, no matter what kind you entered. You can disconnect and denounce any covenant you got involved in by using the name of Jesus Christ.

Prayer (read it loudly)

Father, I come to you in the name of your son, Jesus Christ. I surrender my life to you and everything within me. There are covenants I have involved myself in unknowingly. I ask you to release your power in me, cleanse me and renew me. Every evil force that has been holding me down and stopping me from progressing and having joy, today in the name of your son Jesus Christ, I command that force to loose me and let me go. Enough is enough. I lift my children in your hands; I cover them in the precious blood of Jesus Christ, and I declare that from today as it is written in Isaiah 54:17: No weapon that is formed against thee shall prosper; and every tongue that shall rise against thee in judgment thou shalt condemn. This is the heritage of the servants of the Lord, and their righteousness is of me, saith the Lord.

My Father, Lord, I pray that my children will be a living testimony and they will live to testify the goodness of the Lord in the land of the living. I guard my seed from the wolves of this world. My children will be invisible to the enemy.

Thank you, Jesus, and I believe that from today I am free, and so is my seed. As it is written in John 14:13: And whatsoever ye shall ask in my name, that will I do, that the Father may be glorified in the Son.

In Jesus' mighty name I pray, AMEN.

Chapter 3: Words have power

Words never die. It doesn't matter what is said, when it is said or where it was said. A person may die but the words they spoke will still live with the people who used to hear them.

It matters, too, the position in society this person holds, such as a parent, a teacher, a leader, a friend, and anybody else who can speak and have an audience.

It is very important to be cautious when speaking and know the kind of audience you have.

Dr. Martin Luther King Jr. was assassinated on April 4th, 1968. He spoke some words which up to this day are still alive, and constantly quoted by different speakers. And below are some of the words:

"I have a dream that my four little children will one day live in a nation where they will not be judged by the color of their skin, but by the content of their character."

"Free at last, free at last, thank God almighty, we are free at last."

"Darkness cannot drive out darkness; only light can do that. Hate cannot drive out hate; only love can do that."

"Injustice anywhere is a threat to justice everywhere."

When former president Barack Obama was campaigning, he made speeches and made some statements which people quoted throughout his campaign:

"Yes, we can!"

"We are the change we have been waiting for."

"Change will not come if we wait for some other person, or if we wait for some other time."

"The best way to not feel hopeless is to get up and do something."

"A change is brought about because ordinary people do extraordinary things."

Those words made him so famous, and he won a good number of people's hearts who loved him and voted for him.

President Donald Trump had a famous quote throughout his campaign:

"Make America great again."

Those are words he spoke, and until now people quote him by his campaign phrase.

I can go on and on to quote different people, but all I am trying to bring to your attention is that words have power. They either bring hope or take away hope from people. That's why it is very important to choose the words you speak to others. It doesn't matter who you are talking to. People will always remember you by what you say.

What you speak is greatly influenced by what you feed your spirit, and by your surroundings. The environment you create around yourself, or that which is created around you, in most cases, forces you to speak the way you do. This happens unconsciously whereby you never intend to let the words that come out of you do so. The brain has such power of storage that so many things are stored there - not by choice, but they are there.

Quick question: When do you count the number of times you breathe, swallow saliva, or your heart beats? Never! But all these processes happen inside of you. See, how great our God is, that he created us with a brain, and scientists have identified what they call the medulla oblongata, which is responsible for such activities.

Your determination of transformation begins from the time you get a self-review of who you are. And when you do so, it clearly shows you what you constantly do, and when you identify that which is not pleasant to you, then you change. The same thing happens to the words you speak. Take some time, listen to yourself and evaluate what you say. Has it made a difference in your life? Has it brought you friends or taken them away?

Such questions will help you so much to see where you stand, and then you are in a better situation to transform you to who you desire to be. But it will all start by the words you speak over your life.

What you constantly feed your inner man or your spirit always shows in character. Let's look at it this way: if a person never eats a healthful diet, yet he complains about his health, having high blood pressure, diabetes and obesity, all that needs to be done is to make a change in diet. Then all will be well with the body. It may take time, but persistence and consistence bring results.

What you constantly feed your spirit makes you. What kind of music do you listen to? Rock? Jazz? Dubstep? Rhythm and Blues? Techno? Country? Electro? Or Gospel?

What are the lyrics? Are they soul-building or soul-destroying?

What kind of movies do you watch? Action? Adventure? Animation? Biography? Comedy? Crime? Documentary? Drama? Family? Fantasy? Film Noir? History? Horror? Mystery? Romance? Sci-Fi? Short? Sport? Superhero? Thriller? War?

One question I will ask: the movies you watch - are they helping to bring life to your spiritual man? Do they cause fear? Do they bring career inspiration? Do they cause you to learn anything to help you be useful in the community? A good number of people dress, talk or behave according to what they watch. What do you feed on?

As it is said: You look like what you look at.

Luke 6:45: A good man out of the good treasure of his heart bringeth forth that which is good; and an evil man out of the evil treasure of his heart bringeth forth that which is evil: for of the abundance of the heart his mouth speaketh.

What you say has such a great impact in another person's life, more than what you can imagine. So many times you say a word, and you forget what you said, yet the person you said it to can easily remember it.

Be careful what you say to your child.

When a parent constantly repeats a negative word to his or her child, little does the parent know the kind of impact that word is having on the child. Let's say the child keeps making mistakes and he or she is always told, "You can never do anything right," or, "You will never amount to anything good." Those words are so strong that a child grows up with low self-esteem. These are the people you come across, and they keep asking themselves this question: "What did I do wrong? Everything I do is never successful." It's because there is a word behind, greatly influencing what this person is doing. Unless your spiritual sensitivity awakens and your eyes open beyond the circumstances around you to begin searching the reason for your predicament, it can be hard to have a breakthrough.

In most cases, people tend not to even find out why things happen the way they do. They keep trying one thing after another and all for one reason: "Which one will eventually succeed?"

Proverbs 12:18: There is that speaketh like the piercings of a sword: but the tongue of the wise [is] health.

It is very important to always be conscious of your words when talking, and it doesn't matter what you are saying, either good or bad, but how do you bring it out? What is the reason for your talking? And a question you need to always ask yourself is: "How helpful are the words I am speaking going to be in another person?"

Ephesians 4:29: Do not let any unwholesome talk come out of your mouths, but only what is helpful for building others up according to their needs, that it may benefit those who listen.

As a parent, it is extremely important to always watch what you say to your children. That's your seed, and whatever you speak to them has such influence in their lives. So, you need to pay attention to what comes out of your mouth. If a child makes a mistake, do not be fast at calling him or her these words: stupid, foolish, useless, nincompoop, arrogant, bastard, sloppy, liar, ugly, lazy. Words create and they make things happen. What comes out of your mouth is powerful - you can literally crush a child's spirit, and they are most likely to carry that in them for the rest of their lives.

Quick question: What do you want your child to remember about you? So many times, you come across people who quote words saying: "I remember my mother used to say this to me all the time…" Let the words you speak be remembered as those that build your children's lives, not crush their spirits or destroy their destiny.

Avoid negative statements

Ephesians 5:4: Neither filthiness, nor foolish talking, nor jesting, which are not convenient: but rather giving of thanks.

What you usually call yourself is exactly what manifests in you. It is very saddening to hear people calling themselves names like: I'm a nobody, I'm a nut, I'm useless, I'm stupid, I'm silly, I'm a dummy, I'm poor, I'm a failure, I'm a reject. Seriously, why would you call yourself such things? The devil always uses the words you speak to fight you, and remember the Bible says in:

Proverbs 18:21: Death and life [are] in the power of the tongue: and they that love it shall eat the fruit thereof.

The more you speak negatively over your life, the Bible verse above will surely come to pass in your life. You are probably asking, "Why?" It's the seed you are sowing in your life. So, you will eat the fruit thereof.

Not forgetting that those very negative words you are speaking over your life are seeds, and bad seeds, which fruits you will never enjoy.

Confession is possession.

Galatians 6:7: Be not deceived; God is not mocked: for whatsoever a man soweth, that shall he also reap.

Prayer (read it loudly)

Father, I come to you in the name of your son, Jesus Christ. Forgive me for not seeing the value that you put inside of me from creation. Lord, I spoke words over my life and to those around me that did not edify the spirit man, but caused pain.

I stand in your presence, and I cancel all the negative words that came out of my mouth - those I spoke over my own life, and to other people. Today, I declare in the name of Jesus Christ, the son of the living God, that: Where I spoke hate, I replace it with love. Where I spoke lies, I replace them with truth. Where I spoke destruction, I replace it with newness. Where I spoke delay, I replace it with speed. Where I spoke death, I replace it with life. Where I spoke sickness, I replace it with healing. Where I spoke division, I replace it with unity. Where I spoke failure, I replace it with success. Father, I know you are the God who makes things new. As it is written in:

2 Corinthians 5:17: Therefore if any man be in Christ, he is a new creature: old things are passed away; behold, all things are become new.

I claim this scripture to be at work in my life and the lives of all those I said negative words to, knowingly or unknowingly. From today, I believe there is a new chapter in my life. Holy Spirit, be my guide each and every day, and especially help me to guard my tongue because I want it to bring life and not death.

Proverbs 18:21: Death and life are in the power of the tongue: and they that love it shall eat the fruit thereof.

Thank you, father, for hearing and answering my prayer in Jesus' mighty name I pray, Amen.

Congratulations, as you prayed that prayer, from now on you are a brand-new person. Worry yourself no more over all the negative words that have been a force behind your predicament. God has heard you and answered you.

Speak positively

Do you know that you are God's favorite child? Oh, yes, you are! And do you also know that God has the best plans for you? Of course, he does. If you did not know, as you continue to read this book, you will discover that all you thought you were is less compared to that which God has in store for you. God has so much for you, and the best. For you to start partaking of all those great things God has for you, start speaking great about yourself, and also to those around you. Because even as you speak to those around you, you are sowing a seed and believe me, you want to sow the best seed, so that when the time for reaping comes, you get the best fruits.

Jeremiah 29:11-12: For I know the thoughts that I think toward you, saith the Lord, thoughts of peace, and not of evil, to give you an expected end. Then shall ye call upon me, and ye shall go and pray unto me, and I will hearken unto you.

The only reason why some people fail to enjoy the plan of God is when they fail to use their tongues in a way that attracts blessing to them. It's high time you started speaking and declaring greatness in your life.

Ephesians 4:29: Let no corrupt communication proceed out of your mouth, but that which is good to the use of edifying, that it may minister grace unto the hearers.

Proverbs 16:24: Pleasant words [are as] an honeycomb, sweet to the soul, and health to the bones.

For you to become great it will take you to speak it, believe it and work towards it. Don't imagine greatness and just leave it hanging; every single day say what you want to be and see yourself there. Words like: I am going to make it, I will be great, I will be known by my success, my generation will live greatly. When you declare such words to yourself, it propels you to work hard because you stop looking at yourself in the now but in the coming success.

When it comes to your children, or even another person's child, always speak great things to them. Each and every opportunity you get tell them how smart they are, how good-looking they are, and how you believe in them. When they make a mistake, instead of throwing insults at them, the best you can tell them is, "I know you can do better next time." And as a parent, what you speak to your children means so much to them, and they always hold on to those words for the rest of their lives.

My husband and I decided on one thing, and that is to always remind our children of the greatness that is inside of them, and not to allow anybody make them feel less. This is how we are able to impart boldness in them.

If you are reading and you are a parent or even aspiring to be one, use the principle of positive living in all ways, starting with you and to your children.

There are people out there struggling with identity and acceptance. I don't know if you are one of them, but if so, please stop condemning yourself and looking more at your failures than victories. The potential is inside of you, and from today, start putting it into practice by speaking positively about yourself. Every morning, wake up to a positive declaration. Start with: This is the day the Lord has made; I will rejoice and be glad in it. Do you know how powerful that statement is? It literally sets a pace for the rest of your day, in that it will be very hard for you to be discouraged and you take it in. Why? All things are working for your good. That disappointment may seem to come your way, but guess what! The best is yet to come.

Everyone needs somebody who believes in them, speaks in their lives positively, encourages them, comforts them, cares for and loves them unconditionally. What you say to someone will either build them or destroy them.

This is a true story.

There's this lady who happened to tell her story of her growth and why she made bad choices for a long time. Thank God by the time she was speaking out she had given her life to Jesus Christ and had a transformation. I will keep her identity to myself, but tell you briefly what happened to her. She grew up in a family of twelve children, with a step-dad and an alcoholic mum. She said her parents used to come home late each and every day, and drunk. They would fight and also beat the children as well. She was the oldest of the twelve - ten girls and two boys. Her step-dad kept reminding her that she was a bastard and not his child, and not only that, but he used to molest her in the presence of her siblings. She went on to say that she felt useless and helpless. So, she decided to run away from home and live on the streets where she felt accepted by other homeless people. They introduced her to drugs and alcohol as well. And not long after that, she was also introduced to a cult which promised her to have a better life. To cut the long story short, she became a satanic priestess and lived a life of misery, because the demands were too much. It got to a time when they asked her to sacrifice her own child for a promotion and more powers, and she said she could not do it.

That was the beginning of her life turning around. She ran away, but wherever she went, they would find her, and it got to the point where they wanted to kill her. She moved from state to state until one day when she decided to enter a church to hide, and little did she know that God was looking for her all this while. She says when the service was done, she stayed back to talk to the pastor, and she started telling her story. The pastor started telling her of the pain she was carrying for years and how she was running away from something she thought was supposed to give her joy but brought more misery.

That made her break down in tears, and for the first time she felt accepted and she started to open up to this pastor who gave her attention and time. She could not believe it that there are still people who can give you their time without expecting anything in return. The pastor prayed for her and took her through confession and accepting Jesus Christ as her Lord and savior. He told her to denounce all the covenants she had made before when she was part of the cult.

As she told her story, one thing she kept repeating while speaking was, "I was looking for acceptance and I wanted someone to love me." She lost her identity when she was a child, considering what she went through. There was no one to defend her, love her or take care of her. The pain of being abused and molested by her step-dad had stolen away her true identity. But by the grace of God she was redeemed and transformed. Now she travels and shares her story to encourage people who went through similar situations like hers and were rejected, that there is hope for the hopeless when you give your life to Jesus Christ and make him your Lord and savior.

Whatever you say has an impact, either in your life or in the lives of those around you. And remember, words do not die.

Prayer (read it loudly)

Father, I come to you in the name of your son, Jesus Christ. I am asking for grace each and every day for me to live and speak positively. I am asking for a cleansing of my mind from the past. I am tired of confessing negatively. Holy Spirit, please be the one to help me guard my tongue so that I am able to speak that which is worthy to be spoken and edifies my spirit and all those around me. From today I want to be speaking words that bring life, and I know I cannot do this on my own. I need your help and guidance. Psalm 19:14: Let the words of my mouth, and the meditation of my heart, be acceptable in thy sight, O LORD, my strength, and my redeemer. Thank you, Lord, for hearing and answering me, for this is my prayer, oh Lord. In Jesus' mighty name, AMEN.

Never give up

WINNERS NEVER QUIT AND QUITTERS NEVER WIN.

Nobody wins a race if they stop in the middle, or go all the way, but right before the finish line of victory they choose to sit down. Life is a race and each one of us has got to keep on going, yet nobody knows when they will end this race of life. But we've got to go. Situations can place you in a position of wanting to give up, but you have no choice but to go; it's within the time of the race that you make choices. Either you look back and your pace is slowed down, you look on the right or left to see who is overtaking you, or you look down to look at the marking of the race track. Every action you take during your race has an implication.

As you live each and every day, in this life there are choices we make - almost every minute, from: What to eat? What to wear? Where to go? Who to go with? How long you will spend in a place? Who to talk to? What to watch? What to listen to? Who to get married to? Where to be married? Who comes to your house? And also, where to stay? That is the race I am telling you about, and the choices we make in life. Every choice has an outcome. It is very important to look beyond the current situation when making any choice.

When we were growing up, my mum used to tell us that every action in life has a reward, either good or bad. In essence what she was teaching us is we need to always make sure we make the right choices in every situation.

Making a mistake does not make you a failure. All it does is to make you a better person so that you never make the same mistake again. The problem comes when you continually condemn yourself for the mistake you made. No! No! You do not have to do that to yourself or give up on trying again. It's like a child trying to learn how to ride a bicycle; the first, second, third or fourth time they might fall off, but that doesn't mean that they will never learn how to ride it. A loving parent will say to the child, "You can make it;

let's try again." And before you know it, the child is good at riding his/her bicycle.

Romans 8:1: There is therefore now no condemnation to them which are in Christ Jesus, who walk not after the flesh, but after the Spirit.

Gain trust from your child

A lot of times when children are growing up, they tend to make so many mistakes, and as a parent your role is to correct your child to see to it that they learn from their mistakes and are not blamed for them.

Proverbs 22:15: Foolishness is bound in the heart of a child; but the rod of correction shall drive it far from him.

What this means is that children are innocent in all they do because they do not know how to conduct themselves. It takes the parents to take up their position and train a child. We all grow up by learning. It starts from how to talk, eat, have toilet manners, bathe, socialize, and identify things around us to know the difference between them. So, if parents ignore their responsibility, they are literally neglecting their children.

Proverbs 22:6: Train up a child in the way he should go: and when he is old, he will not depart from it.

I have come across some people who say they love their children so very much, but they never correct them. If you fail to correct your child, you will find that when that child is grown and things tend not to go well (especially when he or she is always making the wrong choices) he/she will blame the parents for not teaching them how to go about life.

To gain your children's trust is very important, and it has to start from when they are still toddlers by creating time for them to talk about what is going on around them, asking them questions about different things, and correcting them when they have done something wrong. It builds a child's confidence in life and it helps them know how to socialize better with other people.

And also, there is a need for a parent to create a parent-child relationship, not for a parent and child to be best friends. There is a thin line. Parents need to stay in their position as parents in order to have authority when it comes to disciplining a child. There is the need of a boundary at a certain extent, yet also to be a friend and a trustee. A child can take a parent for granted if he/she fails on their duties and responsibilities as parents. Disciplining a child varies. Every parent decides in his/her house as seems best.

There are simple, yet important things to consider in disciplining a child (etiquette).

Etiquette simply means a polite conduct or behavior which, if someone practices well, is most likely not going to offend or annoy people.

- Brushing teeth every morning and before bed
- Praying before eating and before going to bed
- Greeting in the morning or when you meet someone you have not seen or even know
- Welcoming back parents from work
- Not talking with food in the mouth
- Maintaining eye contact when talking to someone
- Respecting people in their own caliber
- Respecting elders
- Table manners (eating dinner or any other meal)
- Being polite, especially using words like: Thank you. You are welcome. Excuse me. I am sorry. Please.
- Giving people personal space when need be
- Not talking unnecessarily
- Sitting properly
- Not being loud in public or raising your voice at people
- Proper dressing

The ten commandments are also important to teach a child.

Exodus 20:1-17: And God spake all these words, saying,

I am the Lord thy God, which have brought thee out of the land of Egypt, out of the house of bondage.

Thou shalt have no other gods before me.

Thou shalt not make unto thee any graven image, or any likeness of anything that is in heaven above, or that is in the earth beneath, or that is in the water under the earth. Thou shalt not bow down thyself to them, nor serve them: for I the Lord thy God am a jealous God, visiting the iniquity of the fathers upon the children unto the third and fourth generation of them that hate me; And shewing mercy unto thousands of them that love me, and keep my commandments.

Thou shalt not take the name of the Lord thy God in vain; for the Lord will not hold him guiltless that taketh his name in vain.

Remember the sabbath day, to keep it holy. Six days shalt thou labour, and do all thy work: But the seventh day is the sabbath of the Lord thy God: in it thou shalt not do any work, thou, nor thy son, nor thy daughter, thy manservant, nor thy maidservant, nor thy cattle, nor thy stranger that is within thy gates: For in six days the Lord made heaven and earth, the sea, and all that in them is, and rested the seventh day: wherefore the Lord blessed the sabbath day, and hallowed it.

Honour thy father and thy mother: that thy days may be long upon the land which the Lord thy God giveth thee.

Thou shalt not kill.

Thou shalt not commit adultery.

Thou shalt not steal.

Thou shalt not bear false witness against thy neighbour. Thou shalt not covet thy neighbour's house, thou shalt not covet thy neighbour's wife, nor his manservant, nor his maidservant, nor his ox, nor his ass, nor any thing that is thy neighbour's.

When you choose to train your child with such values, it will not be hard at all for him to cope with other people, because he will know what to do with occurring events of life.

The best way to go about discipline is to correct them each and every time you see them going off, not to give up on them, claiming it's their character. We have a saying where I come from that goes: If a tree grows up bent and nothing is done to straighten it up, when it grows big and you try to bend it, it will just break, not straighten.

In simple language, a child is supposed to be corrected right from birth, and as they grow up, they will maintain the character they acquired since childhood. Never give up on your children, especially when you still have an opportunity to correct them. The potential is always there and you are the vessel the Lord God almighty chose to be the caretaker of his wonderful creation (children). Any parent who gives up on his or her child because of their behavior is surrendering that child's destiny to the enemy. How will they learn if you did not tell them the truth, and how will they correct their own children when they do not know what to do? Think about it. There should be continuity of a generation that makes a difference in a society, and I pray it starts with you to sow the right seeds in your children, so when the time comes and they are parents, they will as well sow the right seeds, and that makes a happy and lasting legacy.

If you are a parent and reading this book, and somehow somewhere you feel you made a mistake when it came to bringing up your children – it's never too late, I assure you. By the time you finish this book, you will know what to do for redemption to come to your family. God loves us all so much that there are always opportunities for us to see his goodness, even in our mistakes.

Prayer (read it loudly)

Self

Father, I come to you in the name of your son Jesus Christ. I am asking you for strength and wisdom to never be quick to judge or give up on myself or my children. Cover me with your love and turn all my mistakes, Lord, into lessons, that I may be able to help myself and other people. In Jesus' mighty name, AMEN.

Children

Father, I come to you in the name of your son Jesus Christ. I stand in the gap for all my children who are going through a time of decision-making. Holy Spirit, please be their guide. I ask you, father, to help me say the right words when talking to them, so that I am able to help them fight the good fight of faith as you lead me. Open my children's eyes, both spiritual and natural, that they may see and know who to trust and not to trust. For the world is full of wickedness, and we can only live in it and fulfill our mandate when you guide us. In Jesus' mighty name, AMEN.

Chapter 4: Be grateful (thanksgiving)

Thanksgiving is an expression of showing appreciation for that specific thing given to someone or an event that has taken place. Different people show gratitude in different ways, for everyone is uniquely created by God.

Psalm 118:1: O give thanks unto the LORD; for [he is] good: because his mercy [endureth] forever.

I will begin by asking a question. How many times have you gone in the presence of God with only thanksgiving? In so many circumstances people go in the presence of God and all they are doing is complaining of how this or that is not going according to their expectations. When things do not work as they want them to, they will ask God why did it not happen as it was supposed to. My question in most cases is: Did you ask God about it before you started doing what you were doing, or did you think it was supposed to be automatic to work out for you? It is very easy to forget including God at the starting point, but later bring him in either in the middle or at the end when things are not going well.

Let me ask this question. Do you take some time every morning when you wake up and say a prayer of thanksgiving for your life and your children, or do you just move according to your schedule?

Every single day, immediately when you wake up, the first thing for you to do is to give thanks to God for the gift of life. Thank him for protection over your household and your children. That should become a habit, like how someone says: "I cannot start a day without a cup of coffee or tea." Let us begin by changing that. "I can never start a day without a thanksgiving prayer to God."

A heart that is full of gratitude attracts the blessings of God. He looks down and sees that whatever he has blessed you with and trusted you with, you are grateful. Look at it in this way; if you are to give someone a gift worth $100.00, and the moment they receive it, they either grab it and say, "I am in a hurry," or, "What is this?" Or, "I didn't know you can give." And that person you have given a gift to does not even say thank you. Would you be in a position to sacrifice your $100.00 again and give to them? Or, you give them that gift, and the next day you find it in the trash. Would you be in a position to give them anything again?

The same principle applies in the kingdom of God. Be grateful so that God can bless you all the more.

1 Thessalonians 5:18: In everything give thanks: for this is the will of God in Christ Jesus concerning you.

Giving thanks in everything means everything, without being selective.

So many people focus on what has not been done for them by God which they have been asking him for a long time, and they turn a blind eye to other things around them that God has given them, or the great battles he has fought for them. If only you could take now just a minute and have a flash back of who you were, what you went through, and how you went through it, and compare it with how you are right now.

I assure you, there is a lot to give thanks for. It does not matter what it was, because the most important thing is God has sustained you and you still have breath to be grateful for.

Look at it this way. You survived that accident. You went through that surgery successfully. You had a safe flight with no plane crash. You escaped that kidnapping; you survived that fire that burned down your house and you came out alive. Those gun shots in the neighborhood did not get to you or your children. That thief that came into your house did not kill you. Those floods did not kill you. Above all you are still alive. Be grateful to the almighty living God.

Psalm 92: It is a good thing to give thanks unto the Lord, and to sing praises unto thy name, O Most High: To shew forth thy loving kindness in the morning, and thy faithfulness every night, Upon an instrument of ten strings, and upon the psaltery; upon the harp with a solemn sound. For thou, Lord, hast made me glad through thy work: I will triumph in the works of thy hands. O Lord, how great are thy works!

and thy thoughts are very deep. A brutish man knoweth not; neither doth a fool understand this. When the wicked spring as the grass, and when all the workers of iniquity do flourish; it is that they shall be destroyed forever: But thou, Lord, art most high for evermore. For, lo, thine enemies, O Lord, for, lo, thine enemies shall perish; all the workers of iniquity shall be scattered. But my horn shalt thou exalt like the horn of an unicorn: I shall be anointed with fresh oil. Mine eye also shall see my desire on mine enemies, and mine ears shall hear my desire of the wicked that rise up against me. The righteous shall flourish like the palm tree: he shall grow like a cedar in Lebanon. Those that be planted in the house of the Lord shall flourish in the courts of our God. They shall still bring forth fruit in old age; they shall be fat and flourishing; To shew that the Lord is upright: he is my rock, and there is no unrighteousness in him.

Enough is never enough

It's amazing how people always make this statement: "I do not have money." Even when they know they have some, it can never be enough.

Money, money, money is the ruler of this world. Mr. Money governs everything done on earth because it is the medium of exchange, and the same Mr. Money destroy relationships, families and lives. Money can easily make you and at the same time destroy you, simply because Mr. Money is always loudly saying one thing. "I am not enough." Even when someone is able to solve all their problems with money, I assure you there are some things money can never mend. As they say, "God made man, man made money, money made man mad."

If only people were grateful for what they have, use what they have wisely and also learn to share with others! Then Mr. Money will be put in a place of: "You are not everything." Deep inside every human being, there is always something missing, and they cannot put their hands on it. And that is the peace of God, and money will never buy peace.

When you look around you right now, you see all that is in your possession, yet you are still looking for more accordingly. Satisfaction (fulfillment of one's wishes, expectations, needs, or the pleasure derived from something) is not on the outside but on the inside of a person. It is very easy to forget what you have and look out for something else - the reason being that's part of the fall of man.

Genesis 2:15-18: And the Lord God took the man, and put him into the garden of Eden to dress it and to keep it. And the Lord God commanded the man, saying, Of every tree of the garden thou mayest freely eat: But of the tree of the knowledge of good and evil, thou shalt not eat of it: for in the day that thou eatest thereof thou shalt surely die. And the Lord God said, It is not good that the man should be alone; I will make him an help meet for him.

Genesis 3:1-7: Now the serpent was more subtil than any beast of the field which the Lord God had made. And he said unto the woman, Yea, hath God said, Ye shall not eat of every tree of the garden? And the woman said unto the serpent, We may eat of the fruit of the trees of the garden: But of the fruit of the tree which is in the midst of the garden, God hath said, Ye shall not eat of it, neither shall ye touch it, lest ye die.
And the serpent said unto the woman, Ye shall not surely die: For God doth know that in the day ye eat thereof, then your eyes shall be opened, and ye shall be as gods, knowing good and evil. And when the woman saw that the tree was good for food, and that it was pleasant to the eyes, and a tree to be desired to make one wise, she took of the fruit thereof, and did eat, and gave also unto her husband with her; and he did eat. And the eyes of them both were opened, and they knew that they were naked; and they sewed fig leaves together, and made themselves aprons.

We see that in the beginning when God created Man, Adam was given authority over everything, and God told him to eat of everything apart from one tree. Even after being given everything, Eve could not resist the temptation from the serpent to eat fruit from that one tree. So, the spirit of "not enough" comes from the fall of man.

Genesis 1:26-30: And God said, Let us make man in our image, after our likeness: and let them have dominion over the fish of the sea, and over the fowl of the air, and over the cattle, and over all the earth, and over every creeping thing that creepeth upon the earth. So God created man in his own image, in the image of God created he him; male and female created he them. And God blessed them, and God said unto them, Be fruitful, and multiply, and replenish the earth, and subdue it: and have dominion over the fish of the sea, and over the fowl of the air, and over every living thing that moveth upon the earth. And God said, Behold, I have given you every herb bearing seed, which is upon the face of all the earth, and every tree, in the which is the fruit of a tree yielding seed; to you it shall be for meat. And to every beast of the earth, and to every fowl of the air, and to everything that creepeth upon the earth, wherein there is life, I have given every green herb for meat: and it was so.

Adam, the first man, was given charge and authority over every living creature.

Most Christians, when they go into prayer, they easily remember what they do not have or what they need, and this is because usually what we need tends to press and put more pressure on us than what we have, which creates an atmosphere of ungratefulness. It is written:

Psalm 100:4: Enter into his gates with thanksgiving, and into his courts with praise: be thankful unto him, and bless his name.

You can easily mistake someone's needs for humility; however, I have come across some people who were very humble at the time they hardly had anything. When God blessed them with money and they were able to sustain themselves better than they used to, suddenly they became very proud, arrogant, selfish and greedy for more. This shows you that even though they physically have material things, they are very poor on the inside. That's why I wrote above that satisfaction is not on the outside, but the inside. Enough is never enough. If you are never grateful for what you have, you will find it very difficult to be satisfied with it, so that the more you get, the more you want.

Nobody keeps a legacy when everything is about them. It gets to the point that their children are not involved in the so-called family business, or even taught how to make money work for them and multiply it to increase. I can only compare money to greed, in that the more you have, the more you need.

It is very saddening to see parents chasing after money more often than spending more time with their children. If a child is detached from a parent, it's like an orphan who has no one to turn to in times of need.

Money can buy every material thing you have, but can never buy time and moments you spend with your child.

I know of a man whose name I will conceal. He was a professor in a known university and he used to lecture in different colleges. Unfortunately, he had no children, although he had so much wealth. The thing that we used to wonder about him was that he never looked like he enjoyed his wealth at all, to the point that he used to drive a ramshackle car. Fate being fate, he died in a car accident. All his wealth was divided among students who needed scholarships, but yet when he was living, he could not help anyone or even give himself the best. So, he left no legacy, because nobody spoke great about him apart from people saying he was wealthy, but lived as a pauper.

So, as you read this book, think more of what others will say about you, especially if you are in a position of helping others, and you fail to. Go an extra mile. Help those in need. Wealth is not about having so much for yourself, but wealth is about being in a position to help feed, clothe and shelter another person. If you do that, then count yourself among those who have enough. For every time you give to someone and they say 'thank you' it releases more blessing to you. It is written:

Luke 6:38: Give, and it shall be given unto you; good measure, pressed down, and shaken together, and running over, shall men give into your bosom. For with the same measure that ye mete withal it shall be measured to you again.

Do not compare children

Every child is different from the other and uniquely created by God. That you can see by looking at the friends you have around you. They are all of different characters, which actually is a characteristic that brings people together without them knowing that the differences bring them together. I have heard several people say they do not like another person copying what they are doing, which shows that different is beautiful.

Look at our finger prints - we are millions upon millions on the face of the earth, and we are all different.

Children are a gift from God. It does not matter how different they are from each other. Always look at your child uniquely from any other and thank God that he will make a difference in the world, because he is different than other children. If you are reading and you are a parent, always avoid looking at other people's children and wishing yours were like them. You may look at them on the outside but you do not know their inside. It's upon every parent to make his/her child extraordinary from other children, by teaching them characteristics that are acceptable in society.

Avoid making comparisons. If your child makes a mistake, you do not have to make statements like, "I wish you could be like your friend," or, "Why didn't God give me the other person's child instead of you?" or, "I wish you were smart like your brother." Such statements make a child feel less than everybody else. In other words, it kills the child's self-esteem.

The more you compare your child, preferring him/her to be like someone else, the more you are destroying them and even taking away that which they are working on to be better people. And it is because they feel that even if they work hard and become better people, you never appreciate it.

As a parent, it's very important to avoid statements like, "I wish God had given me a boy instead of a girl." When a child (your daughter) hears such statements, soon enough they become a tomboy because they think it is what you prefer to have - a boy instead of a girl.

Prayer (read it loudly)

Father, I come to you in the name of your son Jesus Christ. Please cleanse my tongue that I may speak to my children words that make a difference and cause their destinies to be bright. If in any way I spoke anything that has been causing delay and putting hindrances for them not to access their blessings, I come to you as their mother/father and command all those forces of darkness to leave my children's destiny. From today as a parent I decree and declare that whatsoever they will lay their hands on will prosper as it is written in:

Deuteronomy 30:9: And the LORD thy God will make thee plenteous in every work of thine hand, in the fruit of thy body, and in the fruit of thy cattle, and in the fruit of thy land, for good: for the LORD will again rejoice over thee for good, as he rejoiced over thy fathers.

I know God you have heard me and answered me. In Jesus' mighty name, AMEN.

Chapter 5: Prayer direction

Prayer is a mode of communication where we are able to talk to God. And communication is a two-way direction where there is feedback from each party. A lot of times people pray and end up complaining that they are seeing no results of their prayer. My question to you today is: Have you ever heard the voice of God? If yes, hallelujah to that. And if no, then you have the best book in your hands, and start preparing, because I am going to take you through different steps on how you can create an atmosphere of prayer and how best you can have a continuous prayer life that keeps you connected to God.

Do not be deceived by people who say God does not speak. And amazingly, people who make such statements say that they pray. Then whom are they praying to? Probably they have not yet had an experience of the presence of God, to hear from him.

1 John 5:14-15: And this is the confidence that we have in him, that, if we ask any thing according to his will, he heareth us: And if we know that he hears us, whatsoever we ask, we know that we have the petitions that we desired of him.

It's high time you learned how to pray, and also to create an atmosphere that attracts the presence of God. You need to hear God speak, because whenever you are praying, you are speaking to him.

John 10:27-28: My sheep hear my voice, and I know them, and they follow me: And I give unto them eternal life; and they shall never perish, neither shall any man pluck them out of my hand.

Do you know the voice of God? When you pray, you need to also listen, because God talks. Hearing him speak takes your being in the right position so that you can hear him. It is written:

Acts 2:17: And it shall come to pass in the last days, saith God, I will pour out of my Spirit upon all flesh: and your sons and your daughters shall prophesy, and your young men shall see visions, and your old men shall dream dreams:

As you continue to read, get ready because your time has come for you to start dreaming and not forgetting, also to see visions as you enter in the presence of God and are able to hear him speak.

Family prayer altar

Most people hear or read the word altar, and the first thing that crosses their minds is some place made of bricks, and made for sacrifice. Yes, the definition of an altar is a structure upon which offerings such as sacrifices are made for religious purposes.

But a family altar is a place or a time set apart for the family to get together and pray. "A family that prays together stays together." Every time a family gets together, there's a bond that is unbreakable. They start believing in each other and looking out for each other. And when they pray together, chances are that they will never get lonely, depressed, stressed or even die young.

The best way to have a lasting family altar is to set a place in the house and a time which everyone in the house knows and observes. You can have a prayer room, or even sit in a particular place like the living room or dining room. During that time every member of the family should be given an opportunity to read a verse from the Bible, pray, teach, or lead a song. To simplify it for children, you should have a memory verse each week which the children should say every time you meet up for prayer. Begin by teaching them from the book of Psalms. Get short chapters that your children can memorize. I assure you that your children will never live in fear when the word of the Lord is within them. There are times you will not be with your children, and yet they need someone with them. The only friend they have and know that will never leave them is Jesus. They will just get in prayer reciting the psalms they learned, and that's enough to give them strength and stand strong through what they are going through.

In case you do not know what Psalm to start with, let this one below get you started. And by the way, the book of Psalms works for all of us, no matter the age, or what we are going through. It's not only for children. I wrote that you teach your children, simply because it's easier for them to memorize, and also teach them to trust in the Lord and depend on him. Just like how David was in his days - he wrote psalms according to what he was going through. And let's not forget David was a man after God's own heart.

Acts 13:22: And when he had removed him, he raised up unto them David to be their king; to whom also he gave their testimony, and said, I have found David the son of Jesse, a man after mine own heart, which shall fulfil all my will.

Psalm 23

The Lord is my shepherd; I shall not want. He maketh me to lie down in green pastures: he leadeth me beside the still waters. He restoreth my soul: he leadeth me in the paths of righteousness for his name's sake. Yea, though I walk through the valley of the shadow of death, I will fear no evil: for thou art with me; thy rod and thy staff they comfort me. Thou preparest a table before me in the presence of mine enemies: thou anointest my head with oil; my cup runneth over. Surely goodness and mercy shall follow me all the days of my life: and I will dwell in the house of the Lord for ever.

Whenever you are going through a tough situation and you feel completely helpless, go ahead and recite this psalm. You will feel encouraged and uplifted not to give up. You will also be reminded of the presence of God with you because he never leaves us or forsakes us.

When you get together with your family and pray, you are planting a seed of prayerfulness in your children. When they grow up and become independent, they will pick up the same culture of being prayerful in their own houses.

As a family you can decide whether to hold your family prayer altar sessions in the evening or morning. But a time should be agreed upon where all family members who stay in the same house are present.

If your family lives in different places, it would be very good to agree on some dates at least twice a year when you all get together and hold prayers.

During the prayer session, it is very important that every family members' name is mentioned, and everyone presents his or her prayer needs so that they are agreed upon as a family to be answered by God.

In case there are disagreements between some family members, during prayer there is need to pray for forgiveness and reconciliation.

If you desire to have a family prayer altar and you do not know how to begin, pray this prayer of direction.

Prayer (read it loudly)

Father, I come to you in the name of your son, Jesus Christ. Help me to always pray for my family and guide me how to talk to each one of them about the importance of prayer so that when a time comes and we need to get together, Lord, let them agree. Father, give me boldness to speak and help me forgive those who wronged me and touch them as well to forgive me. Holy Spirit, please go ahead of me and lead me. I need my prayer life to change, and that of my family. Thank you, Lord, because I know you have heard and answered me. In Jesus' mighty name, AMEN.

Get a prayer partner

A prayer partner is that person you easily share prayer requests with that you want to agree on. Usually when you pray alone, you can easily give up or fail to pray, because of the situations you are probably going through.

There are times I really want to pray but fail, simply because what I am carrying in my inner man is way too heavy, and it drains the prayerful person inside of me. What I always do is tell my husband to pray, and all I do is agree with what he is praying about. I do not even have to tell him what is weighing me down, but he feels my spirit so drained that he calls me and says, "Sit down here; let's pray." My husband and I are best friends who share literally everything. We had to train our children on the prayer of agreement. When we get together as a family to pray, each one of us gets a turn to pray as others agree. My children always say, "Yes, Lord, yes, Lord, yes, Lord," as another person prays. It shows that whatever the other person is praying about, you agree with them. I encourage you to get a prayer partner with whom you will be having a prayer of agreement.

Mathew 18:19: Again I say unto you, That if two of you shall agree on earth as touching any thing that they shall ask, it shall be done for them of my Father which is in heaven.

On one note, you need to be very careful when selecting a prayer partner. Some people can be your friends, yet they are never for you, although they are with you.

In my book, *You need a Jonathan* (Copyright 2018, Giant Publishing Company), I described the types and kinds of friends that always surround us - fall friends, winter friends, summer friends and spring friends.

There are so many times you can easily mistake these friends by confiding in the wrong one, by telling them your secrets and what hurts you, not knowing that they will soon walk away from you, or, in the worst case scenario, betray you.

Therefore, it is very important to pray about that person that you want to be your prayer partner, since you will be opening up to that person about things that you should not have had to, but because you pray together, you end up opening up to them, because you want them to pray with you or pray for you.

Steps of selecting a prayer partner

What you are about to read is going to direct you on how to choose a prayer partner who will not walk out on you or even start telling others about the things you are praying about. A prayer partner is a very important person in your life, because they literally know everything going on in your life.

1. How long have you known that person?

By the time you choose someone to be your prayer partner, you should be in position to tell who they are. You can never know a person's true character unless you have seen them for a while and gotten to know exactly how they carry themselves, especially around other people.

We all need friends, but you do not want to have a friend who embarrasses you all the time in public by talking irresponsibly and making comments about you which make other people undermine you.

If you have a friend, and for them, nothing is secret about their own lives, then be sure everything they know about you is told to other people., A person who talks so much ends up spilling their own secrets and later accuses others of betraying them. But they forget that they equipped that other person with information which they will use against them and destroy them.

Proverbs 10:19: In the multitude of words there wanteth not sin: but he that refraineth his lips [is] wise.

Proverbs 13:3: He that keepeth his mouth keepeth his life: [but] he that openeth wide his lips shall have destruction.

You do not need a prayer partner who talks a lot. They will even fail to pray, but talk instead. Not only that, but they will tell everyone else of all your prayer requests.

When I ask, "How long have you known that person?" you should be in a position to know that this kind of friend you have will only break you when you tell them something. So, it's better to keep your secrets to yourself.

So, in choosing the right prayer partner, look at the time period you have known that person and their true character. There are those you must watch out for who pretend to be good in your presence, but in your absence, they have a completely different personality (hypocrites).

Someone asked me a question at one time: "Can my childhood friend be my prayer partner, or not?" This can be a yes and a no. Why? It depends on the current walk of your friend. If they are walking with Christ and their ways glorify God, then yes, and the added advantage is you have known them for a long time, so you should know their character.

And also, it can be a no – the reason being if your childhood friend has not given his/her life to Christ to be their Lord and savior. There is no way you can start asking someone who does not even know how to pray to be your prayer partner. It is impossible.

Another thing you need to consider is your conscience. If you feel uncomfortable being with your childhood friend, even though they are born again, then you should not enslave your own mind, because you will not be comfortable at all with them. Sometimes when someone knows you so much right from childhood, they tend to be judgmental in one way or another when it comes to what surrounds you, what you are going through or the decisions you are making. And this is because they will keep bringing the past back of how you used to be or do things - forgetting that days and seasons change. And also, personalities change, since as people we never go through the same experiences in life. And if you are not careful with your childhood friend when it comes to decision making, you might end up consulting him/her while thinking that they know you better. If you do that, you are most likely going to make some decisions which will be regrettable, and in the end, you will blame your friend. Yet partly you are to blame. Why? You should have prayed and asked for the leading of the Holy Spirit.

Lots of people get prayer partners because they hear them talking about Jesus and there and then they open up to them and ask them to be prayer partners. But do you know the character of that person?

Note this: Whenever you come across someone, and in their conversation they talk more about people who they do not like, and they do not like them because of one reason or another, and also they tend to say that God often used them to help such people, be very careful with such a person. Your relationship with that person will not last, because they have a tendency of seeing and quoting negativity about others. So, the way they talk about others, soon enough it will be you. They will always quote themselves as the victims of whatever happened. A constantly negative person can never be a prayer partner because they will end up canceling your prayers.

But if such a person opens up to you when they have recognized their mistakes, then pray for them so that

God can change them. Deep inside of that person, they have a seed of an intercessor, so the devil is fighting that which is within. So that instead of this person praying for others, they are criticizing and blaming others.

James 5:16: Confess your faults one to another, and pray one for another, that ye may be healed. The effectual fervent prayer of a righteous man availeth much.

It will call for you to have a very sensitive spirit to what goes on around you and also go ahead and ask God for a spirit of discernment so that you can see and know who to have as a prayer partner.

Psalm 119:66: Teach me good discernment and knowledge, For I believe in Your commandments.

2. How is that person's prayer life?

Prayer is the master key for every believer who knows they have the supreme living God who listens and answers them. Before you make someone your prayer partner, you should know of their prayerfulness. There are people who say 'I pray' and they actually never pray. Your prayer partner should be part of that prayer meeting you always attend at your church. Observation is very important. When I was eighteen years old, I made a resolution to always be very early at church every Sunday morning, an hour before the service started, to pray for the service. Nobody forced me. I was part of the praise and worship team and had such a great passion to pray. During that morning hour there was another young lady who was also part of the praise and worship team. She could come early, too, for prayer, and I used to observe the way she was praying. The whole hour she was always on her knees and praying nonstop with her head and hands lifted up. I decided to make her my prayer partner because I saw we had something in common, and that was prayer. We were friends before, but not prayer partners. So, you see the difference between a friend and a prayer partner.

When you have a friend who ends up becoming your prayer partner, it's such an awesome thing, because at most times when you eat together you are talking about the goodness of the Lord and how prayers are being answered. I withhold her name for purposes of privacy, but we became so much closer than before, because of prayer. It reached a time that people started calling us sisters, claiming that we looked alike. But it all happened because we were in agreement, both spiritually and physically.

You need a prayerful prayer partner who will not weigh you down, but lift you up in the spirit. Whenever you get together with your prayer partner, even the time of your prayer increases. If at one time you used to pray for five minutes, you improve to fifteen minutes, then to thirty minutes, and before you know it, you are able to pray for an hour and more.

3. How submissive is your prayer partner to the church leadership?

When someone is submissive to their leaders, just know they are humble both in and out. As a born-again Christian, you need a cover and a prayer cover from your spiritual leaders. If someone is always criticizing their church leaders, then that is a rebellious spirit operating in them which opens up to other spirits like disobedience, anger, hate, lies and a Jezebel spirit.

Any person who consistently looks at his/her leaders and sees nothing but faults is a carrier of your downfall when you keep them close to you. Having a person like that as your prayer partner is causing doom to you and by the way, they criticize you, too, in your absence. It is written in:

Psalm 1

Blessed is the man that walketh not in the counsel of the ungodly, nor standeth in the way of sinners, nor sitteth in the seat of the scornful. But his delight is in the law of the Lord, and in his law doth he meditate day and night. And he shall be like a tree planted by the rivers of water, that bringeth forth his fruit in his season; his leaf also shall not wither; and whatsoever he doeth shall prosper. The ungodly are not so: but are like the chaff which the wind driveth away. Therefore the ungodly shall not stand in the judgment, nor sinners in the congregation of the righteous. For the Lord knoweth the way of the righteous: but the way of the ungodly shall perish.

If you walk with a person like that, that is never submissive to his or her spiritual leadership, then you are one and the same with that person.

Amos 3:3: Can two walk together, except they be agreed?

Your prayer partner should be humble enough to respect authority.

Romans 13:1: Let every soul be subject unto the higher powers. For there is no power but of God: the powers that be are ordained of God.

IF you happen to have a prayer partner who discourages you from attending church, but yet encourages you to meet with them for prayer, you need to step away from such a person. The Bible encourages us to gather together as believers, and it is very important because it edifies, encourages and uplifts us as believers in Jesus Christ.

Hebrews 10:25: Not forsaking the assembling of ourselves together, as the manner of some [is]; but exhorting [one another]: and so much the more, as ye see the day approaching.

4. What kind of environment does your prayer partner surround him/herself with?

The things a person surrounds him/herself with on a daily basis greatly influence and determine their character. It starts from friends, music and television shows. If you remember, before you gave your life to Jesus Christ, the kind of life you lived was not pleasant at all. For instance, you used to take drugs, shoplift, fornicate, commit adultery, go night clubbing, were an alcoholic, or any number of other sins.

Galatians 5:19-21: Now the works of the flesh are manifest, which are these; Adultery, fornication, uncleanness, lasciviousness, Idolatry, witchcraft, hatred, variance, emulations, wrath, strife, seditions, heresies, Envyings, murders, drunkenness, revellings, and such like: of the which I tell you before, as I have also told you in time past, that they which do such things shall not inherit the kingdom of God.

As you identify your prayer partner, deeply and carefully look at the manifestations of their behavior/character. If someone still walks in the works of the flesh then it's a no! No! That kind of person cannot be your prayer partner.

2 Corinthians 5:17: Therefore if any man be in Christ, he is a new creature: old things are passed away; behold, all things are become new.

5. Do you know some of the things your prayer partner does outside prayer time?

It is always very good whenever you meet with your prayer partner that you both review the time you were away from each other. Because it is very rare for people to be doing the same thing at the same time, since each one of us runs their daily lives differently.

Your prayer partner is almost your confidante, since you both get to know more about each other – all the more reason you should have the right person who will always uplift and encourage you, and never back bite you.

When you notice something of concern about your prayer partner that is not right, it is best to tell him/her in a loving and caring manner, not criticize one another in public. That kills trust and creates enmity, hatred and low self-esteem.

6. Stay away from a jealous person.

Your prayer partner has to celebrate with you when good things happen.

If you have been having a prayer partner who never joins you for a celebration, consider that person a betrayer and envious. If the two of you have been praying about something, when it happens, you should be able to get together and celebrate.

One time I heard a lady testifying how she was in bondage of the spirit of jealousy. She said that whenever she saw someone buy a new car, buy a house, get a promotion, graduate, or get married, she would become so sick to the point that she felt like killing herself. She went on to say that at times she would hit herself so much and even sleep on the floor, simply because to her every good thing was supposed to belong to her, not the other person. As she was testifying, she said only God could deliver her from the spirit of jealousy, and indeed she was delivered.

So, imagine if you had a friend like that as your prayer partner. That means every time you would come together in a prayer of agreement, he/she would be pretending to be with you, yet in reality would be canceling every prayer, just because that person does not want you to be better than him/her. Jealousy kills; you never want to have it or be with the person who has it.

James 3:16: For where envying and strife [is], there [is] confusion and every evil work.

7. How is your prayer partner's commitment level?

Be observant of what you may consider small things. That person you want to be your prayer partner must show commitment in other things besides prayer time. He/she should be an active member in one or two of the church activities. And when you make an appointment which is outside prayer time, they should be able to keep it. But if it is a person who always has excuses here and there for not making it, then just know that you cannot count on them. People who lack self-discipline are very hard to cope with, because prayer is a consistent habit which forms an individual's lifestyle that portrays the character of Jesus Christ.

Proverbs 25:28: He that [hath] no rule over his own spirit [is like] a city [that is] broken down, [and] without walls.

Prayer (read it loudly)

Father, I come to you in the name of your son, Jesus Christ. I am asking you for the leading of the Holy Spirit for me to get a prayer partner. I desire to have someone with whom I can sit down together and share. I need a Jonathan, a friend who will stand with me, by me and for me, and will never betray me. I have had people come in my life, some of which have left wounds of betrayal, heartbreak, and tears that have taken time to heal. I do not want to go through the same situation over and over. That is why I openly tell you, my Father. You say in your word that you are the father of the fatherless. My Father, I know you are hearing me and going to answer me. Thank you, Lord. In Jesus' mighty name, AMEN.

Write a list of expectations

Take some time, and sit down and write those things you want God to do in your life and in your family.

As a parent, none of your children should be treated differently from the rest. All of your children should feel accepted, so what you need to do is write all your children's names down. If there is a character you see in your child that you do not like or it is not acceptable in society, write down what you want to see happening in your child's life.

All your family members should be part of your success. Write down what your concerns are so that you can pray for them. Some family members may be difficult to deal with because all of us are created differently. As a faith-based believer, keep them in your prayers.

Do not limit yourself to that which looks possible before your eyes. Go for that which other people look at as impossible. Write it down so that you can constantly pray for it.

Like 1:37: For with God nothing shall be impossible.

By writing your expectations, you are exercising your faith, and remember, faith makes things happen. All you do is believe, wait and know that you are getting the answer to your prayer.

Mark 11:24: Therefore I say unto you, What things soever ye desire, when ye pray, believe that ye receive them, and ye shall have them.

In the same way, when you write a to-do list, you are able to accomplish everything on the list. How about if you are only believing and not doing? How exciting is that? Things begin to happen in your life by God using different people to help you, who will see to it that your prayer is answered. Not that they are planning to do so, but the almighty God uses them just for you.

I always encourage people at the beginning of every year to write their New Year's expectations. Whatever they want God to do for them, they write it down. And every prayer meeting they should always pray for everything on the list to see it come to pass. And God, being faithful, I have seen so many people testifying at the end of the year, and when they show you their list almost every item there is marked done, meaning "prayer answered." So, go ahead, write that list, and present it to God; do not fear.

Hebrews 11:1: Now faith is the substance of things hoped for, the evidence of things not seen.

Practice your faith with no fear. God loves people with faith and He greatly rewards them. Your faith in God is able to change things around you for the glory of God.

Hebrews 11:6: But without faith it is impossible to please him: for he that cometh to God must believe that he is, and that he is a rewarder of them that diligently seek him.

Mathew 21:22: And all things, whatsoever ye shall ask in prayer, believing, ye shall receive.

Ask the father our God for what you want. Write your list down and watch him do each and every one of them. At the time you wrote it down, it showed that you believe that God is able to do it.

Ephesians 3:20-21: Now unto him that is able to do exceeding abundantly above all that we ask or think, according to the power that worketh in us, Unto him be glory in the church by Christ Jesus throughout all ages, world without end. Amen.

Are you ready to write? I believe it's a 'yes'. Then you are ready to receive your answer. Get your note book and start writing down what you want God to do for you.

Pray for other families

We have a saying where I come from. "It takes a whole village to raise a child." Meaning, that responsibility in the upbringing of children in the community is for all parents. When a parent notices any unacceptable behavior in a child that does not belong to him/her, he has the authority to discipline the child and also inform the parent of that child's conduct. In some parts of Africa, it's a common and acceptable norm that if a parent finds it hard to discipline their children, they usually take the child to other relatives to help them instill discipline. They do that to teach the children how to behave around other people besides their father and mother. And by so doing, the children grow up with respect and honor for themselves and other people.

But at the speed the world is moving with technology and the law of the land, some of those measures which were applied to discipline children in the old times are no longer as effective as before. The world is becoming more and more corrupt so that you find even relatives no longer trust each other. There have been cases of child abuse, rape and defilement. And the only hope now is to turn to Jesus Christ and by so doing we learn to be our brothers' and sisters' keepers by always praying for each other.

A lot happens in families that you never get to know. You can see by the way some members of the family behave toward each other regardless of who is present. As a born-again Christian, it's high time you stopped concentrating on only your family, and take some time and pray for that family you see is struggling in one way or another. There is a tendency of people looking at their own situations and acting blind to other people's situations. And in most cases, you do not see a change in their families, and yet they say that they are praying so hard. They even start asking God, "Why my family? Why me?" But it is because they have not sowed a seed of prayer in another family.

Every time you pray for another person, you are literally creating a savings prayer account, just like how you have a checking account and a savings account.

If you happen to spend all the money in your checking account and you never deposited any money in your savings account, you will have nothing to use because you did not save.

A savings account is always there for you to deposit money in, and you never use it as constantly as the money in the checking account. Some savings accounts have restrictions, where you are only allowed to withdraw from it three times in a month.

That's exactly how prayer works: you need to have a savings account of prayer. When you cannot pray, you have a deposit of prayer working for you. When the right seed is planted in the right soil, it's just a matter of time before it sprouts out and starts to grow into a tree, which eventually bears fruits, which fruits carry seeds, and the cycle continues.

Every parent should be able to look at other people's children as theirs. If you happen to see a family and their children are getting lost in the world by getting into bad company, remember this verse: 1 Corinthians 15:33: Be not deceived: evil communications corrupt good manners.

Sometimes children can become disrespectful to their parents, or engage in bad habits like alcoholism or drug abuse. God is calling another parent who does not father or mother these children to start interceding for the family which these children come from. The parent praying is sowing a seed of prayer for his/her children.

Pray for your pastor

Your pastor is your spiritual cover who stands in the gap and prays for you. God has assigned your pastor to pray for you and see to it that no harm comes to you unawares. He acts like a spiritual spy; he sees danger before it befalls you and he diverts it in prayer. And the only way your pastor can pray effectively is when his/her spirit is at peace.

I have always wondered why most people, instead of praying for their pastors, do a good job of criticizing them for each and every action they do. Your pastor is your spiritual father or spiritual mother whom God placed in that position for your sake.

Hebrews 13:17: Obey them that have the rule over you, and submit yourselves: for they watch for your souls, as they that must give account, that they may do it with joy, and not with grief: for that [is] unprofitable for you.

Romans 13:1: Let every soul be subject unto the higher powers. For there is no power but of God: the powers that be are ordained of God.

Some people have a tendency of treating their pastors as though they are slaves who are supposed to respond to their call, clap or whistle. You hear a lot about the pastor did not do this or that. They forget that the pastor is also a human being who has a family and goes through trials and temptations. Always be glad to see good things happen to your pastor. It amazes me when you hear stories of certain groups of church members ganging up against their pastor to a point that they want to see him kicked out of the church. I ask myself one question: Who made one man another man's judge? It's not upon us to judge our pastors, but instead pray for them for grace, wisdom, favor, revelation and protection. No man is perfect. Even your pastor is not.

Mathew 7:1-3: Judge not, that ye be not judged. For with what judgment ye judge, ye shall be judged: and with what measure ye mete, it shall be measured to you again. And why beholdest thou the mote that is in thy brother's eye, but considerest not the beam that is in thine own eye?

As you pray for your pastor, fervently pray for his whole family, because when one member of his family is attacked, it affects the pastor's ability to minister. Pastors' children are always a target for the enemy, because that's an effective way the enemy goes through to destroy the church. It makes the pastor not to minister well when his heart is not at peace but constantly worried about his/her children. Yet, the church members look upon him. So always pray for your pastor and his/her entire household.

When you read in 1 Samuel, Eli was a priest in Israel and had two sons, Hophni and Phinehas, who greatly grieved the heart of God by their acts. They always took the best of the sacrifices from the people who came to Shiloh to offer sacrifice to the Lord. And Eli failed to discipline his sons, so that the priesthood was taken away from his family and all the descendants to come after him.

1 Samuel 2:12-18: Now the sons of Eli were sons of Belial; they knew not the Lord. And the priest's custom with the people was, that, when any man offered sacrifice, the priest's servant came, while the flesh was in seething, with a fleshhook of three teeth in his hand; And he struck it into the pan, or kettle, or caldron, or

pot; all that the fleshhook brought up the priest took for himself. So they did in Shiloh unto all the Israelites that came thither. Also before they burnt the fat, the priest's servant came, and said to the man that sacrificed, Give flesh to roast for the priest; for he will not have sodden flesh of thee, but raw. And if any man said unto him, Let them not fail to burn the fat presently, and then take as much as thy soul desireth; then he would answer him, Nay; but thou shalt give it me now: and if not, I will take it by force. Wherefore the sin of the young men was very great before the Lord: for men abhorred the offering of the Lord.

There arose a war between the Philistines and the Israelites, where so many Israelites were killed, and both of Eli's sons, Hophni and Phinehas, were killed. And when Eli heard the news he also fell from the seat where he was and died.

1 Samuel 4:10-11: And the Philistines fought, and Israel was smitten, and they fled every man into his tent: and there was a very great slaughter; for there fell of Israel thirty thousand footmen. And the ark of God was taken; and the two sons of Eli, Hophni and Phinehas, were slain.

1 Samuel 4:15-18: Now Eli was ninety and eight years old; and his eyes were dim, that he could not see. And the man said unto Eli, I am he that came out of the army, and I fled to day out of the army. And he said,

What is there done, my son? And the messenger answered and said, Israel is fled before the Philistines, and there hath been also a great slaughter among the people, and thy two sons also, Hophni and Phinehas, are dead, and the ark of God is taken. And it came to pass, when he made mention of the ark of God, that he fell from off the seat backward by the side of the gate, and his neck brake, and he died: for he was an old man, and heavy. And he had judged Israel forty years.

Eli died and his two sons, and by then God had chosen a prophet whose name was Samuel, Hannah's son whom she asked for, received from, and gave back to God. It is extremely important for every member of the church to constantly pray for their pastors and their children. For destruction can befall the entire church if there is no proper covering.

Be actively involved in a church where people get to know you and socialize with you. It helps a lot in that when challenges arise you have people you can fall back on for prayer and support. Try as much as possible to get involved in different activities that take place at church, especially where you see you have the potential to participate. Things like drama, music, volunteer activities, sports, intercessors, mission team, youth ministry, children's ministry, potlucks, weddings, Christmas or Easter parties, hospital ministry, prison ministry, evangelism, Bible study, and any other activity. When you involve yourself in church activities, you are surrounding yourself with the right people with whom you have the same belief. And it helps you get your mind off any other challenging situations that you may be going through. Don't create a gap for the enemy to come in and destroy you; always keep your mind occupied with things that will build you and not destroy you.

Philippians 4:8: Finally, brethren, whatsoever things are true, whatsoever things are honest, whatsoever things are just, whatsoever things are pure, whatsoever things are lovely, whatsoever things are of good report; if there be any virtue, and if there be any praise, think on these things.

Be committed.

The more you avail yourself in church activities, the more other people in church see you as a committed member. And that means that no matter what you are going through, you can never be alone. You will always have people to stand and support you.

Commitment begins from Attendance, Accountability, Availability and Giving (AAAG). Your blessings can not pass you by when these four (AAAG) things are fulfilled. When it comes to giving, you should be in a position to look unto the Lord and give without focusing on the church or the leaders. Some people do not give to any cause in church simply because they view it as giving to man, not God.

Luke 6:38: Give, and it shall be given unto you; good measure, pressed down, and shaken together, and running over, shall men give into your bosom. For with the same measure that ye mete withal it shall be measured to you again.

Malachi 3:10: Bring ye all the tithes into the storehouse, that there may be meat in mine house, and prove me now herewith, saith the LORD of hosts, if I will not open you the windows of heaven, and pour you out a blessing, that there shall not be room enough to receive it.

Proverbs 3:9: Honour the LORD with thy substance, and with the firstfruits of all thine increase:

2 Corinthians 9:6: But this [I say], He which soweth sparingly shall reap also sparingly; and he which soweth bountifully shall reap also bountifully.

Malachi 6:21: For where your treasure is, there will your heart be also.

Psalm 4:5: Offer the sacrifices of righteousness, and put your trust in the LORD.

Your commitment to church pleases God, and that is a legacy for your generation to come. Your children and your children's children, and your children's children's children, will always quote you as a committed, faithful, prayerful and sold out to God parent. And they will look unto you - that's a seed you plant that will never die, but multiply in your family forever. Look at our father of faith, Abraham. When God spoke to Moses (when he asked him, 'What will I tell people as to who has sent me?'), he told him, *I AM the God of Abraham, Isaac and Jacob/Israel.*

Create a lasting legacy so that your descendants will quote you as a man or woman who feared God.

Honor the church leadership

Every person who is in the position of leadership in your church deserves respect and honor because God has placed them in that position for a purpose.

Romans 13:7: Render therefore to all their dues: tribute to whom tribute is due; custom to whom custom; fear to whom fear; honour to whom honour.

By honoring your leaders, you are sowing a seed. You will also be honored and received. Everything in life begins with a seed; every action you are doing, you are literally storing up what will eventually be done to you. Usually people do hurt others and yet they never want to be hurt. I came to notice that people who usually refer to themselves as in, "That's me; that's how I do it," are never accommodating to others. It's an act of selfishness, yet when it comes to themselves, they expect the best.

God's word is true

Galatians 6:7-9: Be not deceived; God is not mocked: for whatsoever a man soweth, that shall he also reap. For he that soweth to his flesh shall of the flesh reap corruption; but he that soweth to the Spirit shall of the Spirit reap life everlasting. And let us not be weary in well doing: for in due season we shall reap, if we faint not.

Everything you do comes back to you with the same measure. As you give, in the same way you will be given back to.

Luke 6:38: Give, and it shall be given unto you; good measure, pressed down, and shaken together, and running over, shall men give into your bosom. For with the same measure that ye mete withal it shall be measured to you again.

Whatever you give to others you will receive back according to the same measure you give, whether it's hatred, mockery, and despising, or love, care, forgiveness, respect, and honor, that shall you receive. So be careful what you always give to others.

Chapter 6: Prayer groups

A strong church stands on prayer.

1 Thessalonians 5:17: Pray without ceasing.

Jeremiah 33:3: Call unto me, and I will answer thee, and shew thee great and mighty things, which thou knowest not.

It is impossible for a church to be divided when it prays, no matter how many people rise up against it. As long as it is a praying church, it will stand. Church members are empowered spiritually through prayer to fight any battle that may arise to create division in the church.

Ephesians 6:12: For we wrestle not against flesh and blood, but against principalities, against powers, against the rulers of the darkness of this world, against spiritual wickedness in high places.

Having prayer groups should be in accordance with your church policies; this keeps the church in one accord without creating division. If you are to start a prayer group, it is very important to inform the church leadership of your desire to start one and also request for their support. This is called submission.

James 4:7: Submit yourselves therefore to God. Resist the devil, and he will flee from you.

Ephesians 5:7: Submitting yourselves one to another in the fear of God.

Hebrew 13:17: Obey them that have the rule over you, and submit yourselves: for they watch for your souls, as they that must give account, that they may do it with joy, and not with grief: for that is unprofitable for you.

Mothers prayer group

Create or join a mothers' prayer group where all of you get together and start to pray for your homes and children. There are times when you alone do not have strength to pray because of the many challenges you are going through, so by getting together and praying, it uplifts your spirit. This group should be meeting at least once or twice a month for prayer. And also, mothers' retreats are very important because the mothers get away, have fun and get to know each other better. This strongly holds the church together and helps in the upbringing of children. It is in this group where mothers share strength, challenges, solutions and advice.

Mothers are very strong pillars in the church. They nurture and groom the future generation. That's why it is very important for them to keep together as one. I personally was brought up in church, and we used to see our mothers and grandmothers get together after church service. And that act brought us together as children, because we would sit together and wait for our parents to finish their meeting. We would eat together and play together. This created unity in the church. For a church to continue being in existence, it should have women who are dedicated and active members.

Every time you hold the prayer meetings or attend one, write down all the names of your family members and every prayer request. Don't get tired of praying for the same thing over and over – it's okay. Your persistence will cause a manifestation of that which you are praying for.

Marrieds prayer group

Marriage is a union of two people (a man and a woman) getting together as husband and wife.

Ephesians 5:31: For this cause shall a man leave his father and mother, and shall be joined unto his wife, and they two shall be one flesh.

Mark 10:8-9: And they twain shall be one flesh: so then they are no more twain, but one flesh. What therefore God hath joined together, let not man put asunder.

Two people who grew up separately in different families, with different beliefs, norms and customs get to start living together. It comes with challenges because of the different perspectives each one has toward things. And this causes friction, and if not carefully handled, it easily breaks the marriage. I have heard of marriages that last only three months or a year, and then people separate. As I am writing this book, there is this couple that has been married for twenty-five years, with children, and they have decided to divorce. I believe there are certain things they failed to resolve, and as time went on, they could no longer tolerate each other. I witnessed them when they were blaming each other for things that even happened fifteen years ago. It's very sad that people can fail to understand, forgive and help one another when they have stayed together for those many years.

Hebrews 13:4: Marriage is honorable in all, and the bed undefiled: but whoremongers and adulterers God will judge.

The marrieds are a very sensitive branch in church, which ought to be taken seriously, because the enemy always targets the marrieds. When people divorce or separate it not only destroys the couple, but the children too, and the rest of the church body. And this is so because there happens to be a lot of blame and accusation on the man or woman. People tend to judge the couple and blame them for failing to resolve their issues. The children get to be torn apart because they will begin to choose sides as to who is better among their parents, and it creates division in the family.

Married couples need to always meet at church once or twice a month to talk about issues concerning marriage

Topics to discuss in marrieds' meeting

- How to help one another with weaknesses without breaking the person

- How to constantly listen to each other with understanding

- How to patiently deal with the past that tends to always come up in one way or another, like past relationships, or if there are children either of them had before they got married

- Having family prayer altars - this is when all people in a household get together to have Bible study and prayer

- How to raise and discipline children

- How to handle finances

- The importance of sex in marriage

- Why forgiveness is very necessary

- How to divide responsibilities

As a married couple, it is very important to always participate in church activities. That acts like a back-up so that in times of challenges you have people to talk to, and it shows responsibility. If one of you is not able to be in any activity, at least let the other person get involved to represent you. Never separate yourselves from the church and only become Sunday goers. Be there in prayer services and Bible studies.

Husbands, love your wives, and wives, respect your husbands. It is one of the ways that causes longevity in marriage and sets a pace for the rest of your family members, from your own children to the rest of your relatives.

Ephesians 5:22-30: Wives, submit yourselves unto your own husbands, as unto the Lord. For the husband is the head of the wife, even as Christ is the head of the church: and he is the savior of the body. Therefore, as the church is subject unto Christ, so let the wives be to their own husbands in every thing. Husbands, love your wives, even as Christ also loved the church, and gave himself for it; That he might sanctify and cleanse it with the washing of water by the word, That he might present it to himself a glorious church, not having spot, or wrinkle, or any such thing; but that it should be holy and without blemish. So ought men to love their wives as their own bodies. He that loveth his wife loveth himself. For no man ever yet hated his own flesh; but nourisheth and cherisheth it, even as the Lord the church: For we are members of his body, of his flesh, and of his bones.

Youth prayer group

Youth are the future of the church; they are like a spark because of their energy. If they are taught well the word and trained on how to serve God, that is enough to guard them from the wolves of this world. Faith is the shield and the word is the sword. That is why it is extremely important to engage them in different activities at church. If they are left stagnant, they are easily swayed away by bad company. The more they are kept at church and busy, they hardly think about evil.

The problem in church starts from when the youth are not taught how to pray, but how to socialize. Socialization without the presence of the Holy Spirit is like pouring water in a basket. It only goes through, no matter how much you keep filling it with water. Every single week there is the need for youth to meet for Bible study. And as a parent, it is your duty to encourage your children to get involved in church activities as much as possible.

As a church there is a need to have youth retreats or camps where they get to be taught a lot as well as spend time together. I have come across some young people complaining that the reason they do not attend church is because it is boring. Therefore, as an adult or parent that has a home church, go ahead and share ideas with church leaders on how to help the youth.

1 Timothy 4:12: Let no man despise thy youth; but be thou an example of the believers, in word, in conversation, in charity, in spirit, in faith, in purity.

Ecclesiastics 11:9: Rejoice, O young man, in thy youth; and let thy heart cheer thee in the days of thy youth, and walk in the ways of thine heart, and in the sight of thine eyes: but know thou, that for all these things God will bring thee into judgment.

Whenever there's a prayer meeting, every attendee should have a notebook where they write all their prayer requests beginning from their dreams to their inspirations.

What if your child fails to get involved in the church activities? As a parent, start praying for him or her without giving up; eventually they will change. And also engage the youth pastor in what is going on, so that he too can pray for your child.

Singles prayer group

Usually by the time someone says they are single, it's because they are not committed in any relationship. People tend to be desperate, especially if it's a lady who is about twenty-six years old and above, and is not yet married.

Whenever singles get together, they need to pray against the spirit of delay and wrong connections. Praying in unity helps, and since all who gather have a common need, it's easy to have a breakthrough.

Focus prayer points

- Prayer against the spirit of being desperate.

Romans 15:13: Now the God of hope fill you with all joy and peace in believing, that ye may abound in hope, through the power of the Holy Ghost.

- Ask God for the spirit of patience.

Romans 8:25 But if we hope for that we see not, [then] do we with patience wait for [it].

- Pray and cancel all the covenants you made in the past relationships that never worked out. And be fully sold out to God, with no compromise.

Jeremiah 31:31: Behold, the days come, saith the Lord, that I will make a new covenant with the house of Israel, and with the house of Judah.

- Identify all your weaknesses and ask God to help you overcome them.

Psalm 73:26: My flesh and my heart faileth: but God is the strength of my heart, and my portion for ever.

- Ask God to help you with your words. The way you speak always determines how far you will go. Stop confessing negativity, and start confessing positive words.

Psalms 19:14: Let the words of my mouth, and the meditation of my heart, be acceptable in thy sight, O LORD, my strength, and my redeemer.

- Avoid being judgmental.

Romans 2:1: Therefore thou art inexcusable, O man, whosoever thou art that judgest: for wherein thou judgest another, thou condemnest thyself; for thou that judgest doest the same things

- Pray for your husband or wife to be, even though you have not yet met that person.

Ephesians 6:18: Praying always with all prayer and supplication in the Spirit, and watching thereunto with all perseverance and supplication for all saints;

- Pray against and break spirit husbands or spirit wives. If you constantly dream that you are having sex with someone, yet in your waking life, there's nobody, break that evil spirit. It's the cause of your delay. Never take dreams for granted.

As a single lady or man believing and waiting on the Lord for the right spouse, you need to try your best and walk righteously, pleasing the Lord in all ways.

Mathew 6:33: But seek ye first the kingdom of God, and his righteousness; and all these things shall be added unto you.

Using your faith, write down the kind of spouse you want, and the number of children you want. And also, don't underestimate yourself, again using your faith. Draft your wedding budget, putting down the venue of your wedding, the number of guests you want, the color theme, pick your wedding gown, and all the details you want for your wedding.

The advantage of attending a singles prayer group is that right within the group, it is very possible for two single people to identify one another, fall in love and eventually get married.

If you are reading this book and you were once married, and things did not go well and you divorced for one reason or another, do not condemn yourself, but rather, look back at your past marriage and evaluate yourself without judging your past partner. Learn from all the mistakes that were between the two of you that probably led to the divorce. The next step is to start working on all that you have identified in you which used to cause friction in your past marriage.

Continue praying for yourself, be open to learning, rebuke pride and do not let it get in your way. Live in acceptance but not denial, forgive your ex-husband or ex-wife, and above all, forgive yourself. Believe in yourself, have hope, and most of all, have faith. The only true living God who is able to do exceedingly, abundantly above all that we ask or think, is able to connect you to the right spouse whom, if you are a man, you will love, and if you are a woman, you will submit under, and settle in marriage where divorce is never going to be an option, ever, in Jesus' mighty name.

The power of your seed

Hannah cried out to the Lord and asked for a child. God gave to her Samuel, a mighty prophet of the time. When the time came for her to take him to the temple to serve the Lord as she had vowed the day she prayed, she did not take him empty-handed. She knew that her son was going to serve the Lord for the rest of his life, and the only way it would happen is when she offered a sacrifice to the Lord on the day she presented him.

1 Samuel 1:24-28: And when she had weaned him, she took him up with her, with three bullocks, and one ephah of flour, and a bottle of wine, and brought him unto the house of the Lord in Shiloh: and the child was young. And they slew a bullock, and brought the child

to Eli. And she said, Oh my lord, as thy soul liveth, my lord, I am the woman that stood by thee here, praying unto the Lord. For this child I prayed; and the Lord hath given me my petition which I asked of him: Therefore, also I have lent him to the Lord; as long as he liveth he shall be lent to the Lord. And he worshipped the Lord there.

Hannah offered a sacrifice of thanksgiving and sealed her son in the ministry of God to which she had dedicated him. Her sacrifice protected her son from being polluted by the sons of Eli, who by then were misbehaving and disrespecting God while in service as priests.

The Lord gave you children and made you an authority over them to see that they grow up in the fear of the Lord.

Inside of a seed, there's power that causes it to open by itself and allows something new to sprout out. Look at all the plants on earth. They all begin with a seed - mangoes, oranges, paw-paws, and a lot more.

Even the lifestyle we live is based on a seed principle. Every action you take always comes back with its reward, either good or bad. That is why we need to do to others what we want to be done to us.

Galatians 6:7-9: Be not deceived; God is not mocked: for whatsoever a man soweth, that shall he also reap. For he that soweth to his flesh shall of the flesh reap corruption; but he that soweth to the Spirit shall of the Spirit reap life everlasting. And let us not be weary in well doing: for in due season we shall reap, if we faint not.

The principle of a seed is: What you give is what you receive. Show love to others, you will be loved. Hate, and you will be hated. Visit others, and you will be visited.

If you lie, you will be lied to.

Give to others; you will be given to. Don't give, and no one will give to you. Pray for others when they are going through a tough time, and they will pray for you when you happen to go through a tough time.

Visit the sick, and when you get sick others will visit you.

Even when you greet someone, they will respond to you because you greeted them.

Life is about giving and receiving. It's a seed principle.

Life is measure for measure. Matthew 7:2: For with what judgment ye judge, ye shall be judged: and with what measure ye mete, it shall be measured to you again.

Sow a seed for your children, and when doing so, speak over your seed.

How to speak over your seed

Father, I come to you in the name of your son Jesus Christ; by this seed I dedicate my son/daughter into your hands. I separate him/her from all the people whom the enemy had planted in his/her way to destroy his/her destiny. Father, every trap that had been laid for him/her to fall in - I remove it in Jesus' mighty name. Every arrow that the enemy was targeting towards him/her to cause pain, sorrow, delay, disease and rejection, by the power that is in the name of Jesus Christ I divert the arrows now, in Jesus' mighty name. Father, let my seed speak for me on behalf of my children. I cover my son/daughter in the blood of Jesus Christ, and I declare from today as it is written:

Isaiah 54:17: No weapon that is formed against thee shall prosper; and every tongue that shall rise against thee in judgment thou shalt condemn. This is the heritage of the servants of the Lord, and their righteousness is of me, saith the Lord.

Father, open my eyes and show me where, when and what to do as I raise my son/daughter. In Jesus' mighty name I pray, AMEN.

Sow a seed for each and every child of yours, because they are all unique from one another. You may be the parent of four, but each one is different. Cover each and pray for each one of them separately.

If you happen to be going through challenges that never seem to change, yet you continually pray about them, take a step and sow a seed that will speak for you.

I testify about the power of a seed. When I was preparing for my wedding, there were so many hurdles that we had to cross which seemed impossible. Everything was being fought against by one thing or another, to a point that I remember my Aunty asked me a question: Are you sure this man will marry you? I said, yes. I was sure, and prepared to fight, because the Lord had showed me that he was my husband. I went into prayer and fasting for fourteen days, and at the end of my fast, I got a financial seed, went to my spiritual mother and laid it on her feet for prayer. I remember all she said was, "Worry yourself no more, for the chains are broken."

We were forced to changed our wedding date, and that was after we had printed out and already given out our wedding invitations. I went ahead and put in another order for new invitations. I went to my pastor and asked for a change of date. His response was, "We do not do that, but if there is an opening, I will give you a call."

I left his office with assurance that my had God showed me our wedding, and that he had spoken, and no hindrance would stop our wedding. So, I went to my bank account, I withdrew money, and I called my spiritual mother. I did not tell her why I needed to see her, because I knew I was not wrestling with flesh and blood but with principalities. Thank God, she agreed to see me. I actually met her at the gas station and handed her my financial seed. She asked me, "Is everything okay?" I told her, "I am coming with a testimony."

The next morning, I got a call from the pastor's office, saying he needed to see me. And guess what? He said, "Your God really loves you. I have never seen this. Someone came in this morning and cancelled their wedding, saying they needed more time." I shouted, "Gloryyyyyy!" I knew my seed had spoken for me. By the way, previously we were to be wedded at 8:00 a.m. but when the date changed, the time favored us and we were wedded at 11:00 a.m. The power of a seed! Everything went on smoothly, and so many people turned up for our wedding, even after the date had changed.

Never underestimate the power of a seed. We got married, and we still are, and have two lovely boys. To God be the glory.

Never be discouraged when you are going through trials. At that very moment, the name of the Lord will be exalted.

Do not allow fear to destroy your faith.

Your current trial is your tomorrow's testimony.

Your children are your seeds and they will prosper. Protect your seeds.

Your tomorrow will be greater than today, in Jesus' mighty name.

The end

www.ingramcontent.com/pod-product-compliance
Lightning Source LLC
LaVergne TN
LVHW041631070426
835507LV00008B/557